For my

ONE TRUE LOVE

hugs

In love

Purple Ronnie

summersdale

FOR MY ONE TRUE LOVE

Summersdale Publishers Ltd
46 West Street
Chichester
West Sussex
PO19 1RP
UK

www.summersdale.com

www.purpleronnie.com

Printed and bound in China

ISBN: 978-1-84953-877-0

Substantial discounts on bulk quantities of Summersdale books are available to corporations, professional associations and other organisations. For details contact Nicky Douglas by telephone: +44 (0) 1243 756902, fax: +44 (0) 1243 786300 or email: nicky@summersdale.com.

To Sylvia

From Mike

x x

Hollywood Calling

All the stars in Hollywood
Ain't got zip on you
If an A-lister called
to take me out
I'd say, 'Excuse me, who?'

I love you
sooooooo much!

Me being silly on my own...

... Me being silly with you

You always look amazing
You run through
all my thoughts
You're lovely in the
poshest clothes
Or in your shortest shorts!

I don't need Fifty Shades
To get all hot and steamy
I just look at you in
your comfy pants
And shout, 'Come here
and squeeze me!'

Let's take a
duvet day!

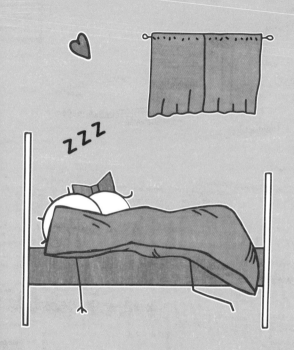

Nights without you...

... Nights with you

You're truly ever
so gorgeous
There's nothing about
you that's duff,

You always surprise me
with choccies and flowers
And say lots of
soppy sweet stuff

I could stare into your eyes all day

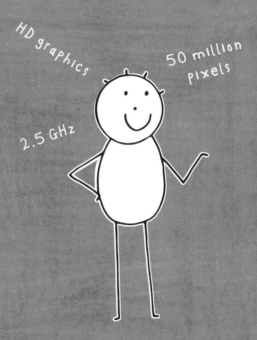

... even if you tried

You know those big rides
at the fairground
When you're queuing
your tum does a flip?
That's just how I feel
when I see you
Excited and happy
(not sick!)

You're cooler than
the sparkliest
superstar celeb

You in your favourite
underwear...

... You in my favourite
underwear

The recipe for our relationship

A sprinkle of mischief
A splash of sauce
A dash of sentimental
And endless kisses
of course!

You give me
the swoons!

You know I think there's
nothing hotter
In the whole wide
world than you
I'd love to spend a
night indoors
With you — and
chocolate too!

I knew you were the one
From the first
time that we kissed
You're a super
five-star fittie
Who I simply can't resist

You're hotter than sizzling sausages!

Remember those
curious fashions
The stuff people
wore in the past?
Our love will be
on-trend forever
Cos it's classic and
tailored to last!

If I were a circus strongman
I'd pump iron every night
But my secret aim in
getting hench
Is to snuggle you all night!

I love how we're
always in tune

Your texts
brighten my day

If I could choose the
perfect date
I know what it would be
A picnic on a sunny beach
And kisses by the sea!

Funsie in a onesie

You look good enough to eat!

I think you're really
smart and sweet
My gosh you sure are funny
Every second spent with you
makes me a happy bunny!

You make me feel

sparkleeeee

You make my heart leap...

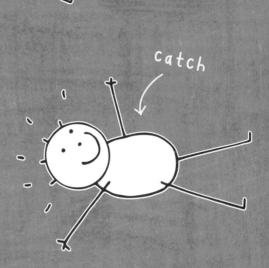

leap

... and other bits too!

I'll say goodnight with
a squeezy hug
And keep you in my wishes
And in the morning
I'll wake you up
With wet and sloppy kisses

#nakedwednesday

If we were marooned
on an island
I wouldn't be bored
for one day
And if anyone came
to our rescue
I'd secretly think 'go away'

AHOY
there

#giftwrapped

How did you get to be so perfect?

I fancy the
pants off you!

I love holding hands
in rain or snow
You're cuddly and
cute and warm
Best of all is snuggling
up close
Cos together we're safe
from the storm

I wouldn't
look twice at
anyone else

picture perfect

Some days I used
to feel lonely
Even with friends
by my side
Now I've got you
as a soulmate
I couldn't feel glum
if I tried!

If we ever have a tiff
I go off and sulk for a while
But I'm secretly planning
the moment,

When we cuddle and
make up in style!

I think you're a
hottie even when
you're snotty
and grotty!

I might not be a
maths genius...

... but I love counting all the brilliant things about you!

I'm taking a minute
to tell you
How totally
smashing you are
Hang on, I'll be more
than a minute
Two hours wouldn't
get me that far!

I'm dazzled by you

Your love makes me
warm and happy
And a little bit
tongue-tied and flustered
You're so flippin' gorgeous
I sometimes feel weak
And my knees go all
wobbly like custard

You always look so luscious
You're never grim or whiffy
If you said 'let's jump into bed'
I'd be there in a jiffy

You're the best
thing that's ever
happened to me!

If we live to be a hundred
We might be grey
and cranky
But I bet we'll still
be in love
(Without the hanky-panky)

coolabi

If you're interested in finding out more
about our books, find us on Facebook
at **Summersdale Publishers** and follow
us on Twitter at **@Summersdale**.

www.summersdale.com